Akampurira Abraham

Microeconomics

An Aspect of Development

Anchor Compact

Abraham, Akampurira: Microeconomics: An Aspect of Development. Hamburg, Anchor Academic Publishing 2013
Original title of the thesis: Microeconomics: An Aspect of Development

Buch-ISBN: 978-3-95489-094-1
PDF-eBook-ISBN: 978-3-95489-594-6
Druck/Herstellung: Anchor Academic Publishing, Hamburg, 2013
Additionally: Business Management and Economics, Uganda, Dissertation, 2013

Bibliografische Information der Deutschen Nationalbibliothek:
Die Deutsche Nationalbibliothek verzeichnet diese Publikation in der Deutschen
Nationalbibliografie; detaillierte bibliografische Daten sind im Internet über
http://dnb.d-nb.de abrufbar

Bibliographical Information of the German National Library:
The German National Library lists this publication in the German National Bibliography.
Detailed bibliographic data can be found at: http://dnb.d-nb.de

© Anchor Academic Publishing, ein Imprint der Diplomica® Verlag GmbH
http://www.diplom.de, Hamburg 2013
Printed in Germany

Contents

Chapter One

1.0 Introduction

Human beings have wants and they are naturally not self-sufficient. They therefore have to produce and exchange what they do not have with those who have what they want. Right decisions have to be made in regard to the quantities to produce and the prices to charge by firms. This is done through the demand and supply theory. Supply and demand in most economies face a lot of challenges. Supply challenges range from small firms with structural supply rigidities to huge firms that act as monopolists and cartels that charge exploitative prices on the consumers. These challenges affect the trading position of several economies in the international trade. Demand is rapidly increasing due to the rapid world increase in population. This paper will cover analysis of decisions of a firm, supply and demand of a commodity, price of a commodity and how the small economic groups and individuals affect the mentioned variables

1.1 Objectives of the study.

The course will;

- Introduce students to important principles of microeconomics so that they are able to take important decisions in life.
- Enable students acquire principles that enable them to analyze day today problems.

Chapter Two

Definitions

2.1 Microeconomics

Microeconomics involves the study of economic actions and behavior of individuals and small groups such as consumers, producers as well as small economic units such as resource owners and business firms. It involves the analysis of the decisions made by individual consumers and firms. It mainly deals with the analysis of price determination which is an emphasis of the market arrangement. Maunder e tal (1996:14) explains that macroeconomics is the study of individual decision making by both individuals and firms.

Economics involves the study of how people and societies use scarce resources to satisfy their wants or needs out of scarce resources. Scarce resources include raw materials, labor, capital energy which aid production and finally fulfills the purpose of satisfying human wants. Society and individual wants include education, medical care, clean environment, and therefore a dire need to have resources to achieve these goals, which unfortunately are scarce. Maunder, e tal (1996), defines economics as the social science of studying human behavior and, in particular the way in which individuals and societies choose among alternative uses of scarce resources to satisfy wants. Scarce resources and unlimited wants lead man to resort to the basic principles of economics that include scarcity, choice and opportunity cost.

Scarcity implies that that there is always a fixed stock of resources that are relatively not enough to satisfy man's needs.

Choice refers to the ability of man to choose from the many alternatives what is best for him. Choice helps individuals or firms to take the right decision while it helps the government to make the appropriate decision and goes on to implement it.

Opportunity cost refers to the alternative sacrificed whenever choice is made. The concept of opportunity cost is important since the resources are not enough to satisfy man's wants at a particular time. During production and consumption, sacrifices are made so that alternative possibilities are foregone because society is faced with a challenge of scarce resources. Opportunity cost is progressively used in the process of exchange where maximum benefit is given up to physical resources such as land, labor and capital.

Scarcity is argued by economists to be a fundamental economic problem. To satisfy individual and society wants implies that they have to choose among alternatives available in order to overcome the fundamental economic problem of scarcity. Economics therefore entails of how choices are made. In line with this Gregory (2012, p 7) says that rational people systematically and purposefully do the best they can to achieve their objectives given the available opportunities. The people across the globe are struggling to work to be better out of the opportunities available to them. In our communities the majority of the people are now awake and therefore the importance of hard work towards poverty eradication and improvement of the welfare.

An economic good is always scarce. The cost of acquiring an economic good is zero. It provides satisfaction relatively scarce and marketable.

A free good exists in natural abundance .Quantity demanded for it is less than supply at zero prices. Economists argue that there are relatively few, if any.

2.2. Production

Production is man's endeavor to use the scarce available resources so as to achieve satisfaction out of them. (Ocan, 2006: 73) defines production as any activity aimed at bringing about a physical change in a good to make it more satisfying and useful. Through the production process, wealth is created and inputs are changed into goods and services meant for human satisfaction. Production entails direct and indirect pro-duction. Under direct production man engages in production in a bid to satisfy one's own satisfaction. Cases are of this production are observed in subsistence production where an individual produces his crops for home consumption. Under indirect produc-tion, firms and individuals engage in production for exchange or sale and money is widely used as a medium of exchange. Therefore to attain maximum benefit, specializa-tion and division of labor is necessary. Specialization and division of labor allows everybody to do what he can at his best since the activity is divided into a series of repetitive tasks and each individual does one task.

There are three levels of production and these include; primary production, secondary production and tertiary production.

Primary production involves man's exploration in the environment to exploit resources aimed at aiding the production process. It entails activities such as hunting, fishing, mining, farming, oil drilling and other extractive industries.

Secondary production involves converting the raw materials into the finished products. It is a stage where value is added to the primary products. Activities involved include textiles, food processing, knitting and embroidery, construction, both on large scale and small scale.

Tertiary production is the stage that increases value on the final product as well as moving commodities from the firms to the final consumers. It is a service provision stage where the goods and services are made available to the consumers.

The overall objective of production activity is to satisfy man's wants. Hard working communities have moved from strength to strength in achieving wealth accumulation and therefore a high standard of living among the respective populations is evidenced. On the hand communities where there is a poor attitude to work, their production levels are low and this seems to be one of the major factors why some areas are still under abject poverty.

2.2.1 Scarcity of factors of production (Resources)

Economic resources are goods that are used to produce other goods or services. These goods are inputs or factors of production. These include land, labor, capital, and entre-preneurship.

Land. Land refers to all natural resources. These natural resources include the gifts of nature which include soil, water, air, minerals, among others. These resources are normally referred to as free gifts of nature because they are natural endowments. Land has a unique characteristic because it is where all production takes place. Land is fixed in supply and subject to the law of diminishing returns.

Labour. Human beings provide labor in terms of physical and intellectual services in the process of production. For production to take place, human resource is needed in labor units employed to the production activity for example drivers, singers, teachers. Labor is a resource that needs to be well managed to maximize returns from it. These include provision of education to improve labor productivity. Also important is health services to have health labor that is able to offer its maximum man hours on the job. Human resource management is vital for human resource planning, training, induction, coaching counseling, supervision, so that units of labor employed are properly utilized.

Capital. Capital is the physical assets that are used in the creation of more goods and services. Capital can be categorized as real capital and money capital. Examples of real capital includes infrastructure, machines, factories, while money capital includes paper notes, coins, stocks, bonds, and other financial assets. They are capable of producing other goods and services.

Entrepreneur. An entrepreneur organizes the production process by planning and organizing factors as well as bearing risk. The entrepreneur has the role of managing and undertaking product risk during the course of production and providing an environment for other factors to operate. Dumba, (2004, p 7), stresses that an entrepreneur has the ability to understand what the market wants which improves his ability to innovate. In addition it is important to note that innovation plays a major role in society development.

6

In the school environment there are many resources under our jurisdiction. These include scholastic materials, human resource that includes teaching and non- teaching staff, students and physical infrastructure. It is important to note that all these resources need to be taken care of carefully because they each contribute significantly towards the school and national goals of education. Staff needs motivation and supervision, students need care, counseling and guidance.

Chapter Three

Exchange system

A barter system is a market system that involves direct exchange of physical goods and services. Much as the barter system may be an effective system in a simple economy, it does not function well in a complex economy where there are multiple production systems. The major loophole associated with a barter system is that any trade requires a double coincidence of wants. This type of trade can only take place if each person wants what the other person is willing to trade and is willing to give up what the other person wants. This has therefore called for use of money system for easy facilitation of trade in almost all societies though with different magnitudes. In some communities of Uganda some people can even work for food. A day's work on someone's farm is equated to some amount of food at the end of the day. Dilts, (2004, p 13), identifies characteristics of the market system that are essential in the allocation of resources which include comparative advantage, division of labor, specialization and capital goods. It is however important that communities where resources are not properly utilized, it is not easy to determine their comparative advantage. Productivity is general- ly not well developed to induce proper functioning of markets.

3.1 Relative and nominal prices

Price shows the value of a commodity at a particular time. This can be reflected in relative terms for instance how expensive this good is by the units of it in terms of units of another. This reflects the opportunity cost of acquiring a good or service in either barter or monetary systems of exchange. This shows how goods and services are either expensive or cheap in relation to others. For a barter system, the relative price means the trading ratio between any two goods or services. For example if one 28 gauge iron sheet is traded for two 32 gauge iron sheets, the relative price of a 28 gauge is two 32 gauge iron sheets.

In a market economy, there are competitive market prices of that are determined by activities of buyers and sellers through the interaction of demand and supply.

3.2 Demand theory

Demand is the willingness of the consumer to buy a certain quality and quantity of goods at a certain price. Demand is greatly affected by the purchasing power. Lack of purchasing power will lead to no effective demand. A population with low purchasing power especially in developing countries has low effective demand.

For a normal good, the higher the price, the less quantities will be bought and the lower the price the more quantities of a commodity will be bought. Quantities purchased by all consumers can be summed up to give market demand. Jhingan, (2006, p 136), stresses that for a commodity to have demand, consumers must have the willingness to buy that commodity, which is related to per unit time. This implies that demand is measurable within a given time after which it changes.

A demand curve is an important instrument to show the price-quantity relationship as shown in the diagram below.

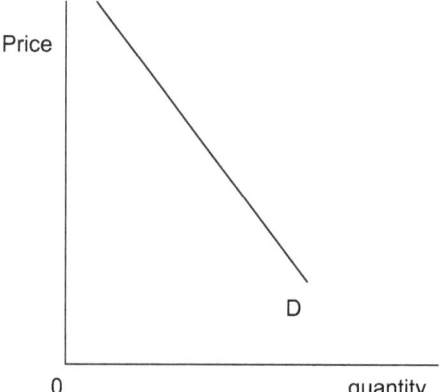

Price

0   quantity

D

The quantity of a good is inversely related to the price of a good, keeping other factors constant. The law of demand is derived from this inverse relationship. The demand curve shown has a negative gradient a reflection of the inverse relationship between the price of a good and quantity demanded in a given time. When prices go up quantity demanded reduces and when prices go down, quantity demanded increases, ceteris paribus.   Other determinants of demand other than price include prices of related goods, level of people's income, the number of consumers, tastes and preferences, expectations of future prices among other factors. The increasing world population for instance has led to increased demand for food, and other basics leading to inflation, hunger and poverty in some communities.

Taking an example of complementary goods, these goods have a characteristic of being bought and used together. For example milk used to make tea will require the house-hold to demand bread as well. An increase in demand for one will lead to the demand for the demand for the other. For substitutes, an increase in the price of X will lead to decrease its demand and an increase in quantity for commodity Y since they are more or less alternative to each other.

Demand for food is increasing at an alarming rate. This is as a result of an increasing global population. Demand for food leads to increased consumption agricultural products. According to Malthusian theory of population, total demand for food is directly proportional to human numbers. It states that population grows exponentially to the extent that resources will be unable to support the available population. This is in agreement of the present situation where there is prevalent hunger in some areas. It is estimated that over 700 million people in the developing world do not access sufficient food, a condition that subjects them to poor health.

There are many determinants of demand which include the following;

a. The relative prices of the goods available

The consumer will demand more of a commodity whose price is relatively lower. The lower prices will attract the consumers while high prices will scare away the customers according to the law of demand. For substitutes like beans and peas, an increase in the price of beans will cause consumers to switch to peas, ceteris paribus, and a decrease in the price of beans will make consumers demand more of the beans. While for the complements like fuel and car, an increase in the price of car will negatively affect the quantity demanded of fuel because there will be few cars lining up on the fuel station for fuel, ceteris paribus.

b. Level of income of income of the consumer

The financial resources at the disposal of the consumer determine the pattern of demand at the existing price, keeping other factors constant. For a normal good, an increase in income is followed by an increase in the demand of a commodity and this reflects a positive income elasticity of demand.

c. Tastes

Tastes and preferences of the consumers influence the demand of a product. Tastes change with the traditions, fashions for and against the product in question leading to a change in the quantity of the product that will be demanded.

d. The size of the population

The size of the population determines how much of a product will be demanded provided that the population has adequate purchasing power and the product in question is within the tastes of the population.

e. Economic conditions

In terms of good economic conditions, the demand of the product will be high compared to when the economy is in bad economic position

f. Seasonal factors

Some products are on high demand for some seasons and this trend tends to   change with changing seasons. Examples of these products include gum boots, umbrellas jackets during the wet season. Their prices tend to be high during the wet season because they are highly demanded in this particular season and their prices fall during the dry season. Shops are highly stoked with these products during the wet season and they tend to disappear during the dry season.

g. The law of diminishing Marginal Utility

D.J. Brown, (1985 : 70) illustrates that if all my shoes are falling to pieces, the need for new ones press a need for buying a new pair- the marginal utility (extra benefit I receive from having one pair rather than none is high for a new pair. Having bought them, however I am quite desperate to obtain the second pair. The marginal utility conveyed by the second pair is less than that of the first. This shows that as more and more of a commodity is consumed, the consumer places less value in obtaining additional unit of that commodity, ceteris paribus.

3.3. Supply theory

Supply refers to quantities that the producers are willing to offer at given prices in a given period of time. Producers are attracted by high prices to supply more quantities to the market while when the prices are low producers will not be attracted to sell since they would want to make profits after covering all the costs of production.

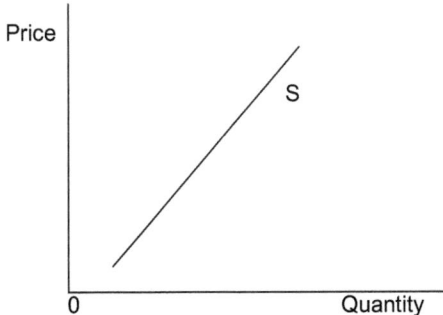

Supply is affected by factors that include the number of producers, the level of technology used in production, availability of capital to employ among other factors. Dumba, (2004, p 31), emphasizes that supply decisions depend on the profit potential. Profit potential induces both local and foreign investors to be innovative a factor that improves supply.

In developing communities, production techniques and limited capital tend to prohibit production levels that affect what is supplied to the market. For instance subsistence production in agriculture that concentrates on production basically for home consumption. Labor is therefore not employed in gainful employment. Others are involved in the informal sector such as shoemakers, tailors, carpenters, vendors and many others where little incomes are earned for bare subsistence of their families. This affects the supply levels to the market, the trading position of these countries and the incomes of the population.

An increase in the price of capital, raw materials and labor resources increases the cost of production and therefore it becomes unprofitable for one to engage in production and supply at the market prices. The on-going price increase in oil products has affected the energy sector and manufacturing sector in countries across the world. It has negatively impacted on supply and made inflation levels to rise in most economies.

Improvements in technology will lead to increased productivity and profitability. This is as a result of reduced production costs and increased labor productivity. This is evidenced by economies of advanced countries such as U.S, China, Japan, among others with high technologies and high productivity.

As in the case of demand, supply decisions can depend on suppliers' decisions. For example, the expected future oil prices may lead to supply less today so that they can stockpile oil products for sale at a later date. On the other hand, an expected fall in the prices will lead to more supply today before the anticipated price reduction.

Providing conducive environment favorable for investment for example a good political climate, favorable macroeconomic policy will improve on the productive capacity of the economy.

3.4. Equilibrium position in the market

In a market economy, the forces of demand and supply determine the price. It is determined at a point where demand and supply curves intersect.

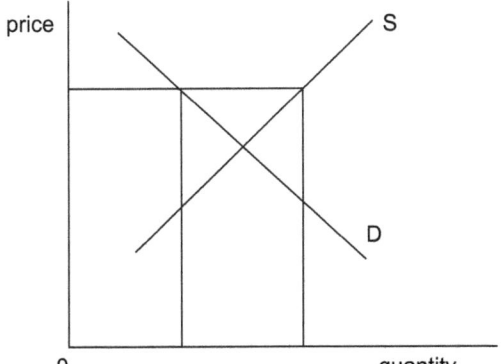

According to Dilts, (2004, p 18), a market is nothing more or less than the locus of exchange. He adds that it not necessarily a place but coming together of buyers and sellers for transactions.

15

3.5. Price ceilings and price floors

A price ceiling is the legal price set such that it becomes illegal for one to buy or sell that price. An effective price floor results into increased resource utilization and reduced excess capacity. This is a result of increased work effort and initiative. Examples of include gasoline prices during the energy crisis of 1970's and rent controls. This kind of price control however shortages that encourage price increase that may end up into inflation. This is illustrated in the diagram below:

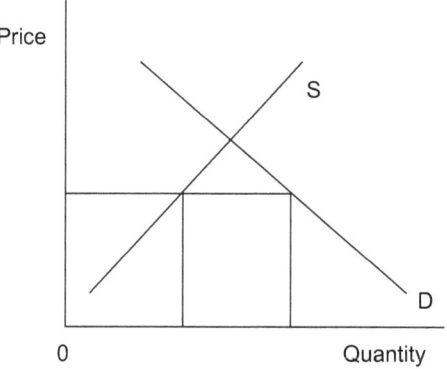

A price floor is a legal set price above the equilibrium below which the consumer is not allowed to buy. Examples of minimum price include the minimum price of agricultural products and minimum wage laws. This is illustrated in the diagram below.

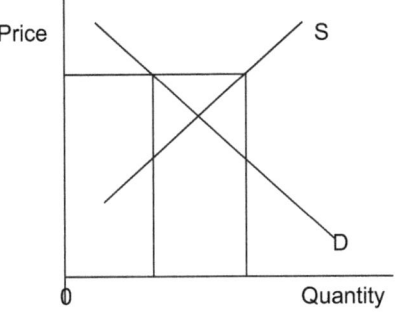

Fixing prices is an important aspect for agricultural development. For instance to guarantee fair prices per unit of output ensures invasions and innovations for agricultural productivity. This increases food production, food security and widen the export sector a prerequisite to economic growth and development.

3.6. International effects

In situations of globalization, firms and other business enterprises import raw materials and finished products from foreign countries. Generally a fluctuation in the exchange rate affects trade and capital inflows and this will have an impact on the standard of living of the people.

Aggregate demand at the regional and international level is comprised of domestic and foreign demand. The foreign exchange rate is the important determinant of foreign demand of a commodity. The price at which a domestic currency is sold to the foreign currency is referred to as the exchange rate.

Chapter 4

Market Coordination

4.1. Markets and the "three fundamental questions"

The three fundamental questions must be addressed regardless the form of economic organization. These include; what to produce, How to produce, and for whom to produce.

- What to produce? In a competitive market economy it is the response of the buyers' and sellers' response determines the mix of goods and services to be produced. More of a commodity that is demanded by the consumers is produced by firms. In our communities it is women who are hardworking, with cash and therefore able to consume women related things. In market places, it is evident that women related items dominate the shops. These include women attire. Hair dressing materials, bangles and rings. Retailers are less interested to deal in men's products.

  Adam Smith, writing in the Wealth of Nations talks about self interested producers. He says that they result in an outcome that benefits all society. In regard to the above argument, he emphasizes that production should be directed towards the society interests. Society interests must be promoted while production and distribution is being undertaken.

This argument suggests that production in a free enterprise economy is always geared to satisfy consumer wants. This forces the firms to produce high quality products that are able to stand competition and this will help to maximize profits as well as provide better services to the consumer. This gives rise to consumer sovereignty where the consumer determines the product mix to be supplied to the market. What is to be supplied to the market   greatly dictates on the production plan. Some economists, such as John Kenneth Galbraith, do not readily agree with above thinking. He attributes the pattern of consumer demand to marketing activities of large corporations. Most economists argue that consumers greatly determine what goods and services they can buy though they feel that marketing methods may influence consumer demand in the short run.

Whenever consumers want to consume more of a good, an increase in demand is experienced, higher prices and this increases the profits of a firm.

- "How is output produced?" This comprises the methods of production and the mix of resources to use while undertaking production. In a competitive market economy, producers do factor combinations that will yield the highest output without compromising the quality. It also involves adoption of new production techniques that aim at reducing the costs of production.

In communities where techniques of production are poor low productivity is experienced. For instance use of hands to till land in agriculture has always led to poor yields, a system that has contributed to economic stagnation in developing communities.

Photo 1 (by researcher on 23/01/2011)

Photo 2 (by Kate on 20/12/2011).

As shown in photograph 1, poor methods of agriculture lead to low productivity. The photograph was taken at Kyanamira 3km from Kabale Municipality. Tilling the land, weeding and harvesting are by use of a hoe. Women still do a lot of work to support agriculture for food security and export. Use of fertilizers and spraying against crop diseases is rarely done. Photograph 2 shows the poor means of transport in the district. Bicycles is the main means of transport to move the produce from farmers to where it is needed. Such conditions do not favor increased productivity.

- For whom? In a market economy, it refers to "who gets what?". In a competitive market economy, sellers and producers are mindful of the market demand before production is done so as to maximize profits. Both output and resource markets are therefore important since resources are needed for production. Better resources receive more incomes for instance skilled labor receive more wages, better land receive more rent such as one that is fertile or in urban areas, better entrepreneur ability receive higher profits. This therefore determines the distribution of income in the resource markets. The nature of income distribution makes the consumers take their own decisions on the quality and quantity of the goods and services to purchase from the output market. In this regard, firms would want to produce for consumers are willing to pay high prices. Needle, (1999, p 275), however notes that some firms use low prices as a marketing strategy. This strategy faces a challenge when there are high production costs that affect the profit level for instance times when the oil prices are high.

4.2. Economic and technical efficiency

Technical efficiency occurs when there is full employment of resources. There are no resources that are unemployed or underemployed. In this case production is along the production possibility curve.

It must be noted that any change that benefits someone negatively affects or results into harm for someone else. This is catered for under economic efficiency. Both economic and technical efficiency are achieved when production is done along the production possibility curve.

A seller is able to compare the returns from selling a good or service and continued possession of the item being sold before he takes the decision of selling it off. On the other hand a buyer decides on buying an item or alternative items that could be purchased with a given monetary payment. Economic efficiency occurs when all trade possibilities are explored to tap all potential gains.

4.3. Consumer equilibrium

A consumer is faced with many feasible alternatives among which he can derive the highest level of utility. He has to work within a fixed level of income that he has to spend on alternative combinations of goods and services. A consumer has unlimited wants but his money income is fixed. In order to maximize utility, the consumer will select the bundle of goods at which the following two conditions are satisfied:

1. $MU_A/P_A = MU_B/P_B = ... = MU_Z/P_Z$, for all commodities (A-Z), and
2. all income is spent.

If the consumer derives more satisfaction from good A than from good B, he will substitute the latter for the former until their marginal utilities are equalized. Given that each commodity has a price of its own the consumer will allocate his income on the respective on the budget; A, B, ... the unit of currency spent on each good or service gives him the same marginal utility. Consumer equilibrium is said to occur when the above conditions are satisfied.

The challenge that is faced in the developing countries is that most of the people do not have any income. This applies to the unemployed and the aged who are unable to work. It is also important to note that some people in most economies do not use cash for survival. They depend on local gardening and local natural resources for food and energy. They rarely depend on going to the market for their needs. Consumer equilibrium in this case is difficult to determine using the above model.

4.4. The role of price mechanism

Price mechanism is a system of economic organization in which each individual i.e producer, consumer or resource owner is engaged in economic activity with a large measure of freedom. It is a free enterprise system where there is a large freedom to privately own resources. The market forces of demand determine the allocation of resources through the price system of the goods and services. There is therefore "allocation efficiency" of the available resources in the economy.

Price mechanism helps to answer the fundamental economic questions i.e what, how much and for whom to produce. The system determines what the consumer wants so that the resources are allocated in a similar direction to avoid a wastage of resources.

Resources are allocated to production of commodities which the consumer wants. How much to produce is answered by how much a consumer is able to consume in a particular period. Less is produced if the consumer is able to consume less and vice versa. The mechanism of how to distribute the commodities once they are produced is also addressed so that all feasible distribution channels are determined.

Price mechanism helps to in the allocation of the resources. In a free market economy, resources such as land, labor and capital are allocated where they fetch high prices and high profits.

Price mechanism helps to determine the distribution of income. There is a flow of income from resource owners to producers and also to consumers. Those who own more resources will earn more and those who own few resources will earn less. The urge to own more resources creates a motivation towards innovation, hard work and research.

Price mechanism plays an important role as a motivator to economic growth. The dire need to acquire more wealth and profit generates encourages work effort, new and better techniques help in accelerating economic growth.

Maunder, e tal (1996 : 58) stresses that in many parts of the Western economies much of the decision making that goes on about what, how and for whom is carried out in markets by voluntary exchange.

The system however presents a challenge where the existence of the monopoly limits the smooth operation of the price system. Consumers do not have adequate information about the quality of the products visa-vis their prices in the market and where the products are available. Also the price system may not be efficient where there are varying income social groups and the needs of a particular group are ignored by the producers.

The price system does not take into account provision of essential services to the community such as clean water, primary health care, roads which call for direct government involvement to provide these services.

The price system poses a challenge where the private benefits prevail over the public benefits. Therefore there is a profit motive at the expense of the natural environment management. Negative effects to the environment such as deforestation, overfishing and pollution result. Lipsey (1979: 357) stresses that when the owners of the factors maximize monetary gains from the factors, it will have a negative effect on convenience and good climate.

Chapter Five

5.0. Market Failure

To ensure effective trade, there should be no market imperfections. These hamper the markets from achieving economic efficiency. These results into market failure and these include imperfect information, externalities, public goods, merit and demerit goods, inequality and the absence of property rights, monopoly and imperfect information. According to Frank Livesey (1995: 97), stresses market failure exists when resources efficiently by the market mechanism. It can result into high costs of advertising and other forms of product differentiation a state of inefficiency in resource allocation. He adds that this can occur in both highly concentrated and low concentrated markets.

The weakness of the market mechanism is that is fails to efficiently allocate resources which results into disparities of income among the population thus a gap in wealth and living standards.

5.1. Imperfect and inadequate information

Sellers and buyers need complete knowledge on the market conditions for effective use of the market. Whenever there is no complete knowledge, sellers and buyers may not optimally gain. For instance when they do not know the prices at which goods are being sold or quality of the product being bought and sold. An example is lack of information of second hand cars by the potential buyers when the sellers have more knowledge about it. This can lead to market failure since it can destroy market for second hand good quality cars.

5.2. Externalities

While production takes place, externalities result. They are social costs and benefits that accrue to a society from a market activity. Some result in social costs that affect the welfare of society. There is however a positive externality where society benefits for example a farmer who keeps bees amidst other famers. These other farmers will benefit from the bees through a process of pollination. In such a case subsidization is neces-sary to beef up such a farmer. Government can correct the situation of negative exter-nality by setting up regulations for example a limit on the level of chemical and com-pound emissions that are released into the atmosphere. Taxation is also another strategy available by government to reduce these on activities that yield externalities for example high taxation on cigarettes to reduce on the rate of smoking.

Another example is where firms were requested by the U.S government to provide accurate and complete information to ensure safety standards of public. Incidents of unsafe drugs, and other consumables is declining in the United states. In the developing world, lack of information about the product market and work places lead to public welfare loses. Government regulations and policies should aim at protecting the citizens with a lot of commitment from all the stakeholders.

5.3. Inequality in society

This is a condition where resource allocation among the population is not even. Where-as some people will have enough resources, others are economically suffocated with hardly any resources. It is the role of government and society to ensure that all people benefit equally on the national resources. Measures such as taxation and minimum wage legislation are used by governments to protect the unprivileged in society. It is however important to note that some of these measures lead to market failure. For instance minimum price legislation may cause market failure since leads to unemploy-ment.

5.3.1. causes of income inequality

Disparities in wealth among the population is very common in the capitalistic economic reasons. This is due to

- Differences the resource endowments and other economic opportunities is on of the reasons why there is a wide gap between the rich and the poor. Some areas are naturally endowed with rich minerals and other resources giving an advantage of the population therein to have better incomes and high standard of living. The type of employment where some labor engage in well paying job compared to their counterparts.
- Differences in education and training that brings about diffences in skills puts the educated in a better position to earn higher than the uneducated. Those with lower incomes tend to have lower incomes, limited access to medical care, clean water, adequate nutrition and general poor welfare.

- Inheritance is another reason for the existence of income inequality in most communities. Some people have their origin in a rich family background that puts in an advantage of accessing economic opportunities compared to those that hail from a poor family background.
- Segregation and discrimination on the religious, tribal, sex or political grounds creates unfairness in the resource distribution. This is especially so when there is weak government policies and poor policy implementation.
- Differences in the natural ability and talents makes the highly talented to earn higher incomes compared to the less talented.
- Income inequality occurs in societies because some people work hard while others have a negative attitude towards work. In some societies, men have left most the work to women who are therefore unable to bail families out of poverty. These women are not necessarily highly trained to have high productivity.

It is however important to note that income inequality can be addressed through regulatory and structural policies. These include implementation of fiscal policy through progressive taxation, minimum agricultural prices and subsidies, allocation of social economic infrastructure even to rural areas, provision of free education and training so as to empower the population socially and economically.

Chapter six

6.0. The decision of a firm

A producer turns inputs such as land, water, raw materials into output. The aim of the firm is to minimize the cost of production. The firm opts for the cheapest factor combination that yields a given level of output. Guogiang TIA, (2006, p6), stresses the importance of analyzing the economic situation to make trade off choices to determine the equilibrium position. For the case of a firm, this is a point where the firm makes profits.

6.1. Profit maximization

Profit maximization is the major of objective of most firms. They therefore minimize the costs of production to maximize profits. Total profit is the excess of total revenue over the total cost.

Profits allow entrepreneurs to expand the firms since more production factors will be purchased to increase the level of output. Making losses may force the entrepreneur to divert the resources to another industry. Under perfect competition, more profit will ensure that efficiency is achieved. Profits will increase on the capital and this is reinvested in production.

6.2. Total revenue, Marginal Revenue and Marginal Cost of a firm

Total revenue: This is the total amount of money that a firm realizes from the sale of its total product.

Economic profit = total revenue - economic costs

A profit maximizing condition is where MC=MR. This implies that a firm is in equilibrium when the marginal product is equal to the marginal product per unit of currency spent on labor.

6.3. Profit maximization under perfect competition

Under perfect competition, each buyer or seller has no control over the market. A producer being a price taker and faces will horizontal demand curve for its product.

At the level of output (Qo) at which MR = MC. This is a point where the firm maximizes profit. The price, Po, is determined by the firm's demand curve. A firm produces at output level of Qo.

Since he faces total costs equaling to ATCo, his profit per unit of output equals to the shaded area. (= revenue per unit or output - total cost per unit of output)= P_O-ATC_O.

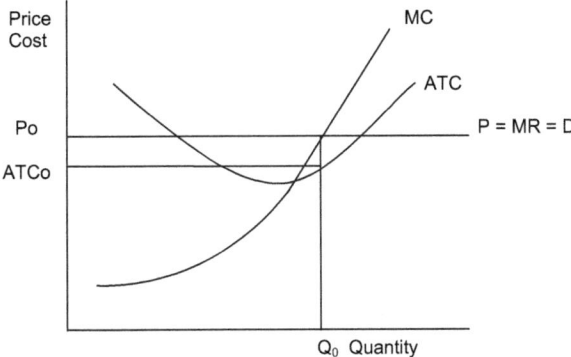

6.4. Profit maximization under the monopoly market structure

A monopolist maximizes profits at a point where MC=MR. At this point the monopolist

charges price OP₀ and this is a point where the output line meets the demand (AR)

curve.(the demand curve of a monopolist is inelastic). The intersection of the MC and

MR curves intersect at the equilibrium of the firm. This is at the output level Qo. The

price that firms can charge to sell this much output is given by the demand curve. This

price equals Po.

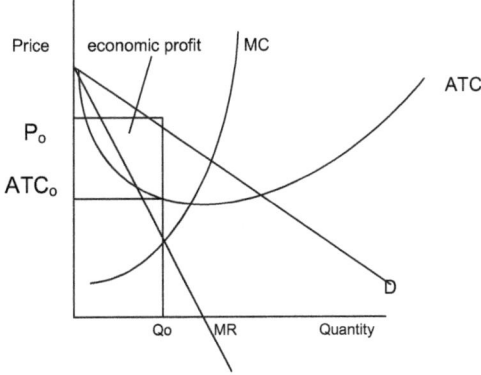

The monopolist firm earns abnormal profits as shown by the shaded area in the diagram. These profits are equal to the .Difference between the price and the average total cost is equal to the abnormal profits enjoyed by the monopolist.

Multinational co-operations have practiced monopoly powers across the world especially in the developing countries. The result has always been high commodity prices, lack of choice by the nationals a situation that negatively impacts on the welfare of the people across the world.

6.4.1. Sources of Monopoly

A firm can emerge as a monopolist and develops powers to prevent entry of other firms into the industry. The basis of monopoly is built on the following factors.

a). Patent right.

A patent is a legal right given to the producer of a new product that prevents entry into the industry of other firms from producing the patented product for a certain period of time.

b) Government protection.

The government strategy to protect the domestic production against imports, can make some firms obtain artificial monopoly powers.

c). Nationalised Industry.

Nationalized industry arises out of government take over of the private firms in an industry through the act of parliament.

d). Take over's and amalgamations.

This arises out of firms coming together to form one unit with a stronger base so as to tap the economies of scale.

e). Franchises.

These firms thrive out of the government directive to give these firms monopoly powers to cater for this product. This can be done through licensing or patent so that when this firm obtains monopoly power, it can be more efficient in service delivery once the firm invests in technical innovations.

f). Geographical Integration.

The firm can obtain the monopoly powers because of the location in which the business enterprise is located and this type of integration can have horizontal, vertical or lateral elements.

6.4.2. Price discrimination.

Price discrimination is a practice of selling the same product or service to different consumers at different prices by the monopolist regardless of the costs of production incurred. Lipsey ,(1978: 267) emphasizes the conditions under which a firm can suc-ceed in charging discriminatory prices are, first that it can control what is offered to a particular buyer, and second, that it can prevent the resale of the commodity by one buyer to another. In addition other conditions found out to make price discrimination a success include;

   a) *Effective separation of the market.*

There should be a possibility of sub dividing the market into different sub markets with different price elasticities. In the service sector it is easier to organize this market arrangement than a market with goods.

b) *Market imperfection.*

Price discrimination works very well where there is some degree of imperfection in the market since there are barriers of entry into the industry.

c) *Geographical barriers.*

Price discrimination may base on the geographical location of the consumers. e.g. discrimination between domestic and foreign buyers.

d) *Age.*

Age makes it possible for the monopolist to discriminate against different consumers for example charging low rates for children and high rates for adults at a stadium for a show.

e) *Sex/ Gender.*

It is possible for the monopolist to do discrimination customers on the basis of sex. For instance; low rates for ladies and high rates for gentlemen on disco halls.

f) *Nature of the product.*

Discrimination is possible with products that have limited or no close substitutes.

g) *Personal income.*

Price discrimination is possible among different income groups for instance medical doctors' services to the rich and the poor on a discriminatory basis.

Price discrimination helps the producer to raise more revenue because of increased sales. It also helps to increase the welfare to all members of the society since the same commodity is available to people of different social and economic settings.

6.5. Other market structures

Other market structures that need to be examined include monopolistic competition, and oligopoly. Perfect competition and monopolistic competition is characterized by many firms with freedom of entry and exit into the industry. However under monopolistic competition there is a lot of product differentiation that is non existent in perfect competition.

A good example of a monopolistically competitive market is telecommunication sector in Uganda, and the restaurant market in New York City.

Competition among firms is so important in the sense that it stimulates new and desirable ways of doing things. This results into better product quality and increased consumer choice. Environment is an important aspect the market. According to Needle, (1999, p5), environment includes all elements that exist outside the organization and interact with it. They occur at the local, national levels. There is competing environment at the local level where firms offer the same product in the same market. At the national level there is influence of the government policy while at the international level multinational co operations interchange business ideas across the globe.

6.6. Employment and output

A bigger number of the unemployed resources negatively impact on the level of production. Frank Livesey, (1995 : 170) stresses that higher employment means a higher output of goods and services, an indicator of satisfactory economic performance. For labor as a factor of production however, firms may shed labor in order to reduce costs making labor redundant. The increasing number of unemployed on the globe is an indication of the idle resource that would be helpful in production if it was properly tapped. There are several sources of voluntary unemployment and in this case labor supply is greater than labor force in the economy. Some of these include:

Some people who have just finished schooling may want first to enjoy some leisure before they seriously engage in active work. In this way labor will not be willing to work during this time period. This is however not common in the developing world because of the poor family back ground. In some communities where there are social security benefits, job search may not be taken as an urgent task.

A deficiency in demand pauses a threat to the employment sector. Frank, L. (1995: 172) stresses that lack or deficiency of demand has been a major cause of unemployment in the UK over the past two decades. Deficiency in demand have always caused alternate slow economic slow down and this impacts on the rate of unemployment.

Loss of competitiveness of some economies in the international markets lead to the unfavorable terms of trade and this makes the price of exports to fall in relation to the price of imports. A loss of market for exports discourages investment leading to unemployment.

The inappropriate education where the curriculum emphasizes theoretical disciplines that are not relevant to the real society experiences makes the school drop out fail to be innovative in their own environment. Uncontrolled birth rates and increased population pressure will strain the available resources and therefore saving is discouraged and this affects investment. High illiteracy rates seem to be part of the causes of high population growth rates that is not planned for.

Distribution of economic activities and wealth that is not even especially between urban and rural areas causes a gap in employment capacity for different areas. Government and private investments tend to concentrate in the urban areas, a situation that aggravates rural urban migration. There is in addition uneven distribution of social services such as health care, education institutions, and general conditions of life that appear better in the urban areas.

To increase output it is important to improve on the employment of resources. A special attention should be paid to rural development policies especially in the developing countries. This entails agricultural modernization, infrastructural development, controlling population growth rate and this enhances investment thus reducing unemployment. This therefore calls for respective governments to design policies to bail communities from peasantry and subsistence agriculture so as to create employment and increase output.

Encouraging industrialization through provision of a conducive investment climate creates jobs in addition to providing market for the agricultural produce. More people would be employed in the agricultural sector once it is commercialized to meet the demand of feeding the industries with adequate inputs.

Unemployment has adverse effects in the respective economies and serious implications on the economic growth. Some of these effects include low output and low incomes. Incomes of the people are low due to lack of jobs and this impacts on the aggregate demand which consequently affects investment. The jobless lose self-esteem , confidence, recognition and human dignity in society. Due to low or no incomes, they have nothing to contribute to their homes and societies and end up being total dependants. There is a high possibility of high crime rate when large numbers of the population are unemployed and this leads to political instability.

6.7. Regulation

Regulation helps to protect the consumers against the unfair treatment by the producers. Some regulation has been done across the globe for instance during the earlier years of these industries, the U.S. regulated the airline, trucking, and railroad industries. This was done to avoid the unnecessary competition that hinder the growth of firms especially those that are still in infancy. Frank Livesey (1995: 98) identifies licensing as the most common form of regulation. Licensing protect participants especially in the financial markets against irresponsible and unscrupulous behavior. Licensing however becomes tricky in a situation where there are many businesses the informal sector. Other forms of regulation include nationalization .With nationalization the government can undertake the business activity in a bid to protect the consumers. A monopolized entity will reduce waste in the form of costs of duplication with the competing producers.

6.8. Resource markets

In the resource market the economic reward for land, labor, capital, and entrepreneurship are rent, wages, interest and profit respectively. Profits are made after the entrepreneur has met all the costs of production.

The circular flow diagram describes the relationship between output and resource markets. Households are resource owners and therefore firms purchase resources from households in resource markets. On the other hand, firms supply output to the households. It is however important to note that there is an important interdependence between output and resource markets. The interdependence between output and resource markets is so vital in the production process products.

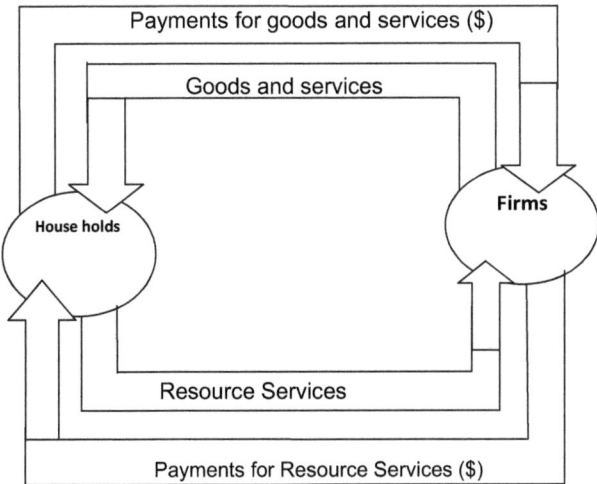

The circular flow diagram shows that the households are the source of supply of resources in the resource market and firms are the source of demand in the output market.

6.9. Natural resource markets and environmental policy

Natural resources comprises of nonrenewable resources and renewable resources. Nonrenewable resources have a finite supply that is depleted as the resource is consumed. Producers have the ability of replenishing renewable resources. Examples of renewable resources include: timber, land, agricultural products, cows, among others.

Extraction of the nonrenewable resources *is* determined by need to meet economic human need without considering other aspects of development such as preservation of ecology and biodiversity. For example the rate of drilling oil depends on the price offered in the market. There is a time preference on when to supply nonrenewable resources. Micheal, P. (2003), emphasizes that rising pressures on the environmental resources in developing countries can have severe consequences for self-sufficiency, income distribution, and future growth potential in the developing world.

Environmental degradation and its ills can cause stagnation in economic development through reduced productivity of resources. It is estimated that 20% of the world's population will be affected by environmental degradation practices greatly. Population pressure on the marginal land has affected food security and per capita food production which lead to a perpetuating process of the interaction between poverty and the environment.

6.10. Allocation of resources and environmental problems

When the price reflects all the marginal costs and benefits, then the market will allocate the resources efficiently. Externalities cause market failure. One example is environmental pollution. This happens because the marginal cost of the activity exceeds the marginal private cost. Lack of private property rights for resources results into environmental damage. This includes environmental pollution, deforestation among other environmental damages. Gregory, (2012, p 3), emphasizes that a society must allocate resources by deciding by who should do what in addition to allocating output of goods and services. This calls governments to empower local governments to allocate resources in order to achieve sustainable development.

6.11. Economics of the family

The households have an important decision to make of the number of children to have. It is noted that in developing countries, children are a source of labor for household chores and agricultural production while in developed economies; children provide consumption benefits to their parents. In communities where fertility rate is still very high, there is a high dependence ratio that strains the little incomes earned at the household level. This limits the savings which leads to low investments and persistent poverty. Also noted with concern is the child bearing rate after the World war 11 when men and women had been separated during the war. This led to rise in fertility rates between 1946 and 1961 with outstanding consequences. From that time fertility rates have reduced because the people would like to catch up with better lifestyles.

Ensuring proper income distribution leads to emancipation of the families. It improves the purchasing power thus increasing the socio demographic characteristics of then population. Lifespan improves and the family sizes reduce. Savings improve and this increases investments.

6.11.1.Subsistence production

Subsistence production is one where the individual or household undertakes production mainly for ones own consumption. It is characterized by production for household use and therefore the household needs hardly go beyond the basic needs of life i.e food shelter and clothing. Traditional methods of production are applied using the rudimentary tools such as axes, hoes, pangas and therefore the quality and quantity of output is low. AEObone. (1984 : 140), explains that the level of agrarian technique is exceedingly low and tools and equipment are both limited and primitive in nature. There is no specialization and division of labor leading to lack of innovation and invasion and consequently low productivity and skilled manpower development. There is little exchange and once done it is though barter system. The productivity of the sector is very low and this leads to low capital accumulation.

6.11.2.The Market (Monetary) production

This is a form of production where production is profit motivated and it is therefore done on the commercial basis. Modern methods of production are applied using modern tools and inputs and therefore high productivity many job opportunities are created. There is specialization and division of labor which encourages research, innovations and inventions. Skilled labor force is used which increases output for sale and this widens the export sector which improves the balance of payments position of a country. Economies of scale are such as marketing, transport, supervision, technical economies are en-joyed.

6.11.3. Agricultural price fluctuations

Agrarian communities face fluctuations in income as a result of fluctuations in prices. This is mainly caused by unplanned and exogenous changes in supply. Richard Lipsey (1979: 140) explains that output coming onto the market at any one time is the result of production decisions taken in the past, while decisions taken about production in the present will not have their effect on the quantity supplied until sometime in the future. This trend in the market affects both producers in terms of incomes and consumers in terms of prices. Other pertinent factors that drive the market conditions include the supply lag that is brought about by the long gestation period of the agricultural products. By the time these products reach the market, they may not necessarily address the demand that they were originally meant to.

6.12. Forms of Business Organizations

Business organizations are business enterprises that are involve in the production and distribution of goods and services.

1- **The private sector.** This includes all privately owned businesses. Examples are;

   a) The sole proprietor.

   b) Partnerships.

   c) Joint-stock companies.

   d) Private Limited companies.

   e) Public Limited companies.

2- The Public Sector. This includes all businesses and undertakings which are owned by the state e.g Uganda Posts and Telecommunications, Uganda Electricity Board and other parastatal bodies.

2- **Joint ventures** are owned by both the government and the private sector.

3- **The community sector** e.g cooperatives.

The Soleproprietor.

This is where the business is owned by one person and therefore generally referred to as a one man business. It involves a small-scale operation where he manages the business personally at times with the assistance of the members of his family or hires an assistant. He has all the powers of controlling the business and must take appropriate decisions in regard to the business operations. He funds his business through personal savings and borrowing.

Advantages of sole proprietorship.

a) The business is easier to start since it requires small capital. One starts immediately after mobilizing little organizational costs and at times securing a license.

b) There is efficiency since the owner has full control over the business. The decision making process and implementation is faster.

c) There is little resource wastage since the owner has to be very careful to avoid making losses. Personal supervision ensures that resource wastage is minimal.

d) The owner develops good rapport with the clients since he has direct personal contacts with the customers.

e) The ability to organize his business encourages hard work since he does not share profits with anybody.

Disadvantages of the sole proprietor.

a) The owner of the business is personally reliable to the debts incurred. He has unlimited liability. i.e. when the business collapses, it will not only affect the assts of the business but also his private assets and property therefore there is no distinction between the owner and the business.

b) There are limited finances available for investment. The sole proprietor has a challenge of raising the required capital alone.

c) The business depends solely on the entrepreneur. It can even collapse after the death of the owner.

d) The owner is over worked because he is the sole controller of the business. He works for long hours and cannot get time to relax.

e) It may not be easy to secure loans from financial institutions because he cannot easily be trusted.

PARTNERSHIPS

This is where two or more people agree to share responsibility and pool their resources and carry out business jointly. Members in a partnership are usually between 2 and 20 who come together and join hands for the sake of having the their objectives realized. Capital contribution, profit sharing and any other issues pertaining the running of the business is spelt out in a partnership deed which is presented to the Registrar of businesses before the partnership starts.

Advantages of a partnership

a) Partners can easily raise more capita to run the business compared to sole proprietorship.

b) Partners combine and develop capital and management ability to run the business.

c) Specialization and division of labor is possible in the process of running the business e.g. sellers, transporters etc.

d) Business may continue after the death of one of the partners because of joint involvement of many stakeholders.

e) Sickness does not affect business operations as the case with sole proprietor.

f) The burden of bearing the liability is minimal since it is shared among the partners.

Disadvantages of the partnership

a) Partners have unlimited liability as with the case of sole proprietor with the exception of some partners who may be limited partners and hence have limited liability. Otherwise, each partner is liable for the debts of the firm.
Therefore the liabilities of the partnership can extend to the personal possessions of the partners.

b) All partners will bear and own a mistake committed by one of the partners.

c) The profits realized may not be encouraging because it has to be shared between or among the partners.

d) Partners may have diverging interests and therefore liable to disagree in decision making .

e) The hard working partners contribute and profit realized is shared among all partners. This is in most cases affect the work effort.

f) It is characterized by delays in decision making and this affects the running of the business.

JOINT- STOCK COMPANIES

These are business organizations where the owners are shareholders with a purpose of carrying out business. The board of directors do the duty of making policies and hiring management. The business is a separate legal entity from shareholders since it can own property, sue or be sued and make contracts. Shareholders have limited liability. They are liable to the debts of the company only up to the share capital. The possessions of the shareholders cannot be sold to meet the debts of the company even if the company is indebted. The nature of the business and the way business is conducted are well laid down in the tow documents namely; The Memorandum of Association and The Articles of Association. Promoters present these documents to the registrar of companies. For a public limited company, a document called a prospectus is published by the promoters to invite the public to apply for shares so that capital is raised from sale of the shares..

A limited company can be a public limited company or private limited company. The major differences are as shown in the table below;

Private Limited	Public Limited.
1. Minimum number of members is two people. 2. Maximum number of members is 50 3. Shares not freely transferred without the consent of members.	1. Minimum number of members is 7 2. No maximum number of members. 3. Shares are freely transferable and bought or sold in stock exchange markets

Advantages of Joint- stock companies

a) The sale of shares makes it possible to raise enough capital to run the business.

b) Members have limited liability i.e. when the business fails to clear the debts, they lose their share capital. Their personal property is not encroached on.

c) The company continues to exist even when one or some of the shareholders die.

d) A company has more capacity to access loans from financial because of enough collateral securities.

e) In cases of losses, they are shared among many shareholders.

Disadvantages

a) Shareholders do not exercise direct control of the business since technical staff is hired on their behalf.

b) Some shareholders tend to dominate decision making since they hold more shares.

c) It is a long process and very expensive to form a company because it requires many procedures.

d) Decision making and implementation tends to be very slow since a lot of consultations have to be made.

e) There is almost no secrecy in business especially public limited companies where all accounts are always made public.

CO- OPERATIVES

Co-operatives business organizations formed by members who come together to achieve and share the benefits together. They organize themselves for the purpose of benefiting the members.

Types of cooperatives

a) Marketing cooperatives.

b) Consumers cooperatives.

c) Credit and savings cooperatives.

d) Producer cooperatives.

e) Transport co-operatives.

Principles of cooperatives.

a) Democracy is exercised through voting on the basis of 'one man one vote'.

b) Open and voluntary membership; nobody is prohibited to join the cooperative provided he is able to pay the membership fee.

c) Limited or no interest on share capital i.e. members do not share all profits earned because no interest is paid on the share capital contributed by members. Where profit is made, it is used to expand business.

d) They are financed by members.

e) They are supposed to observe impartiality i.e. they should not interfere in politics, religion or race.

f) Education is supposed to be provided to the members .i.e. traders, farmers depending on the type of the co-operative in question.

The role of cooperatives in Development

They help farmers to transport and market farm products e.g. coffee, maize etc.

They help to provide farmers with cheap inputs like fertilizers, hoes, tractors etc.

They help to transform the economy through participating directly in agriculture and industry.

They provide education to members, and to the public e.g. on how to adjust to new methods of agriculture, how to use fertilizers, new tools and new methods of farming.

They help members access get credit to use in the business enterprises. Co-operatives also help to mobilize funds from Development Banks and other financial institutions.

They provide employment to many people in transportation, marketing and export of their products.

They increase unity and cooperation among the people for a common cause. In some countries, co-operatives have acted as political units especially in social countries.

Consumer co-operatives protect the interests of the consumers and provide them with cheap consumer goods. They buy in bulk, sell to members at low prices and sell at high prices to non- members.

They eliminate exploitation of farmers by middlemen.

Chapter Seven

7.0. Recommendations

Economies should aggressively address unbalanced growth and income inequality in communities. This involves building community capacity through skills, investing in infrastructure which can enhance increased incomes.

The trend of government expenditure should be aimed at sectors that benefit the citizens such as education, agriculture and infrastructure. These sectors need government support especially in Africa, Asia, and Latin America. Government expenditure in these sectors was reduced due to structural adjustment programs. Such endeavor improves the primary health care, reduce poverty for improved purchasing power and enhance development for increased resource utilization.

Government policy to improve household energy consumption use should be emphasized. This will improve the people's welfare as well as protecting the biodiversity and ecosystem. Households need energy for cooking, heating and lighting among other domestic uses. Energy consumption patterns should be planned for at the national and global level. It is noted that average per capita household energy in the developing world is still very low. It nine times less than their counterparts in the developed world.

Governments should emphasize on the capacity building of the communities. This can be done through helping the people to create self employment through providing basic skills to the people and extending credit facilities to the poor and the landless. Such people do not have the capacity to access credit in financial institutions due to lack of collateral security. Such program helps community members to start income generating projects and this helps to reduce poverty levels.

Environmental considerations should form an integral part of policy initiative. There should be inclusion of environmental costs while calculating GNP.

Chapter Eight

8.0. Conclusion

Microeconomics deals with the study of decisions of a firm, supply and demand of a commodity, price of a commodity and how the small economic groups and individuals affect the mentioned variables. Production in the developing world still faces supply rigidities. These include transport bottleneck, inadequate government subsidization, poor techniques of production, among other rigidities and these negatively affect productivity in the developing world. Production and consumption decisions are also affected by imperfect information, externalities, absence of property rights and monopolistic tendencies. These affect quality and quantity of production, prices in the market, the health of citizens and utilization of resources. The paper covered aspects of microeconomics among which include the behavior of consumers and producers and the decisions they take, market coordination, the effect of production and consumption on the environment among other issues.

Nations should address the unemployment problem that is negatively impacting on society. This can be done through human resource development where the population is equipped with relevant information and life skills so as to use the environment and the resources to make their ends. Local initiatives are necessary to promote entrepreneurship acumen that would increase investment opportunities through mobilization of resources for productive activities. Desirable policy reforms to facilitate growth of the leading sectors in the economy are needed to propel the entire economy into the right economic path.

References

AEObone. (1984).*Economics. Its Principles and Practice in Developing Africa*. Edinburgh : Clark Constable.

Ayres, Robert U. (2005). *On the Reappraisal of Microeconomics : Economic Growth and Change in a Material Change*. New York : Edward Elgar Publishing, Inc.

D.J. Browne (1985). *Economics for 'A' Level*. Singapore: Toppan Printing Co.(S) Pte Ltd.

Frank Livesey, (1995). *A Texbook of Core Economics*. London : Longman.

Hamanaka, (2009). *Asian Regionalisation and Japan : The politics of Membership in Regional Diplomatic, Financial and Trade Groups*. New York : Taylor & Francis Routledge.

Harvie, Charles. (2005). *Sustaining Growth and Perfomance in East Asia : The role of Small and Medium Sized enterprises*. New York : Edward Elgar Publishing, Inc.

Hoe schele, Wolfgang. (2010). *The Economics of Abundance; A Political Economy of Freedom, Equity, and Sustainability*. UK: Ashgate Publishing Ltd.

John Dumba. (2004). *Basic Economics for East Africa*: *Concepts analysis and application*. Kampala : Fountain Publishers.

Lavoie, M. (2010). *Money and Macro dynamics* : Alfred Eichner and Post- Keynesian Economics. New York : ME Sharpe, Inc.

Maunder , e tal (1996). *Economics Explained*. 3rd edition. Musselburgh: Scotprint Ltd.

McNally, David.(2011). *Global Slump : The Economics and Politics of Crisis and Resistance.* Texas: Spectre.

M. L. Jhingan, (2002). *Microeconomic Theory.* Delhi : Vrinda Publications (P) Ltd.

Michael, P. (2003). Economic Development. (eighth edition). Delhi: Pearson Education (Singapore) Pte. Ltd.

Walker, Donald. A. (2006). *Walrasian Economics.* London: Cambridge University Press.

Guoqiang TIAN, (2008). *Lecture notes on micro economic theory.* Texas: A & M University.

Richard G. Lipsey (1979). *An introduction to Positive Economics.* London: Harper and Row.

MankiN (2011). *Principles of economics.* USA : Nelson Education Ltd.